Oh, What A Joy is A Solar Eclipse
Written by Jessie Silbert and Jon Silbert
Illustrated by Jessie Silbert
Published in the United States by Celestial Buddies, LLC Guilford, CT 06437 USA
Printed in Shanghai, China
FIRST EDITION
ISBN: 979-8-9877757-0-7
UPC: 793888861138
SKU: CB086

www.CelestialBuddies.com

Oh, what a joy is a Solar Eclipse!
Your Buddies will guide you with How-to-View tips!

But where can I go see a Solar Eclipse?
You can see it from planes; you can see it from ships!

You can see it from water or see it from air.
A Solar Eclipse can be seen anywhere.

Fact: A solar eclipse can only take place during a "New Moon," when the Moon's path passes between the Sun and Earth and is therefore not visible because Moon's illuminated side is facing away from Earth. A solar eclipse occurs every 18 months or so somewhere on Earth, but because 71% of the Earth's surface is covered by water, it is quite rare to glimpse a total eclipse on land.

Although you won't see one from far out in space,
You __can__ see the shadow it makes on Earth's face

But to see one in flight or at sea is a wish
That's more probably granted to birds or to fish!

Fact: On August 21, 2017 millions of people viewed a total eclipse from Earth. Meanwhile, 250 miles above the Earth, six people . . . the Americans Randy Bresnik, Jack Fischer and Peggy Whitson, the European Space Agency's Paolo Nespoli, and the Russians Fyodor Yurchikhin and Sergey Ryazanskiy . . . watched from the International Space Station as the umbra passed over the Earth. It was certainly an amazing view . . . but the best place to see an eclipse of the Sun is still right here on Earth!

Image Credit: NASA

So what all this means is, when all's said and done,
It's on land that you'll see an eclipse of the Sun.

Hi, Buddy,
come down here! You
won't want to miss this!

Fact: Because more than 70% of the Earth's surface is water, an eclipse is far more likely to occur over water than over land. But land is where we human beings live, so it is on land where we people are most likely to see an eclipse of any kind.

But it does have to be at the right time and place,
When our Moon in the daytime obscures our Sun's face.

Astronomers calculate dates and locations
From which we can view these celestial sensations.

And show all of us a spectacular sight:
As the brightness of day becomes darkness of night.

But there once was an era when nobody knew
How eclipses occurred...believe us, it's true.

Fact: As a solar eclipse reaches totality, the temperature drops and the breeze dies down. You can see stars and planets. Animals that are active during the day return to their homes, thinking it is night. Nocturnal animals (those that are normally active at night), such as bats and raccoons, may come out. Although confused by the sudden darkness, however, the animals all go right back to what they had been doing once the eclipse ends and the Sun comes out again. You will notice, however, that human beings won't be able to stop talking about what they have just seen!

And the people on Earth hadn't quite figured out
How this strangest of solar events came about.

A long time ago people tried, we have heard,
To explain in their own way just what had occurred

In China they thought that a dragon came by,
And it gobbled the Sun from its place in the sky.

Fact: The Chinese were not the only ones who believed an eclipse was caused by the Sun's being devoured. In Vietnam, people believed a frog swallowed it. Ancient Mayans believed a snake ate the Sun, while the Vikings thought the culprit was a giant wolf.

Greeks and Egyptians and Aztecs and Romans
All feared that eclipses were really bad omens.

Fact: In ancient times, a solar eclipse was seen as a bad sign. The word "eclipse" comes from the Latin "eclipsis" and the Greek "ekleipsis," meaning "to fail to appear." When the Sun "disappeared," many people thought they had done something wrong and that their gods were abandoning them.

Because ancient peoples had not been enlightened,
The Sun's disappearance would make them feel frightened.

And think that eclipses were omens of war
Or of famine and pestilence, sickness and more.

Fact: Many ancient people thought that eclipses came about because they had somehow offended their gods, such as Zeus, the Greek King of the gods; Huitzilopochtl, the Sun god to whom the Aztecs made human sacrifices to keep the sun moving across the sky; Ra, the Sun god of the ancient Egyptians, who believed Ra drove his barge across the heavens during the day and descended into the underworld at sunset; and Apollo, who was a Sun god to both the Greeks and Romans.

Fact: Eclipses have been happening long before people were around to see them, but the first known written record of a total solar eclipse comes from 1223 BC, more than 3,000 years ago. It was documented on this clay tablet attributed to a Bronze Age Civilization living in Ugarit, an ancient port city on the northern Mediterranean coast of modern-day Syria. Some people, however, think that some mysterious carvings on a rock in County Meath in Ireland might have been intended to show an eclipse that occurred more than 5000 years ago!

Without any warning the sky would turn black
There'd be no way to know if the Sun would come back.

Astronomers Studying an Eclipse (1571). Antoine Caron (1521-1599)

So what DOES cause eclipses? I guess you will ask.
And the answer to that is your Buddies' next task.

Image Credit: NAS

Who's better to ask than our Earth, Moon and Sun?
Explaining eclipses for them is great fun.

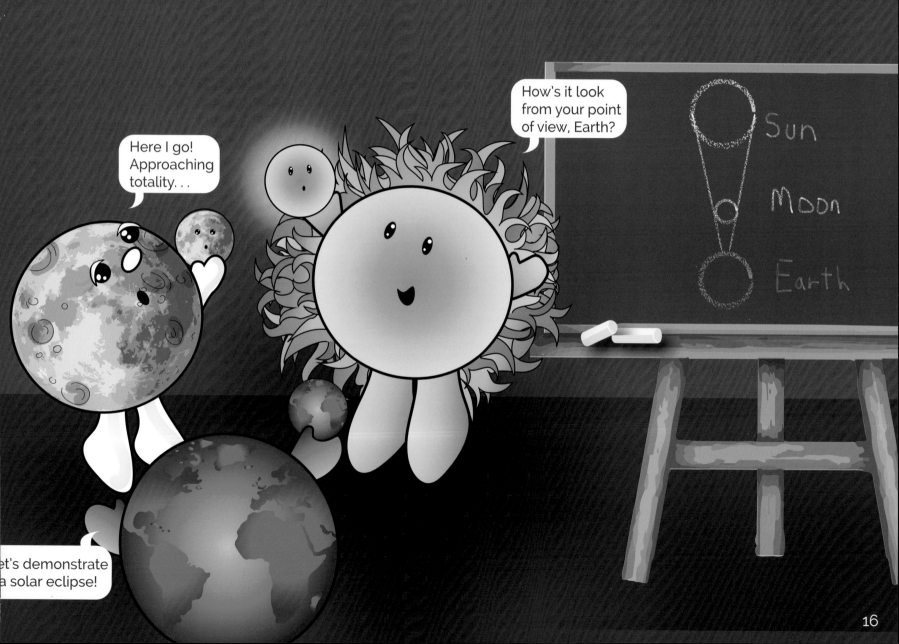

**Science provided the true explanation:
Your Buddies will give you a neat demonstration.**

Hey Moon,
What are you
doing?

Just passing through!

Fact: A Solar eclipse occurs when the Sun and the Earth line up with the Moon between them. The Moon blocks out the Sun's light and creates a shadow on the face of the Earth. Solar eclipses only occur during a New Moon when the Moon is not visible from the Earth because its illuminated side is facing the Sun.

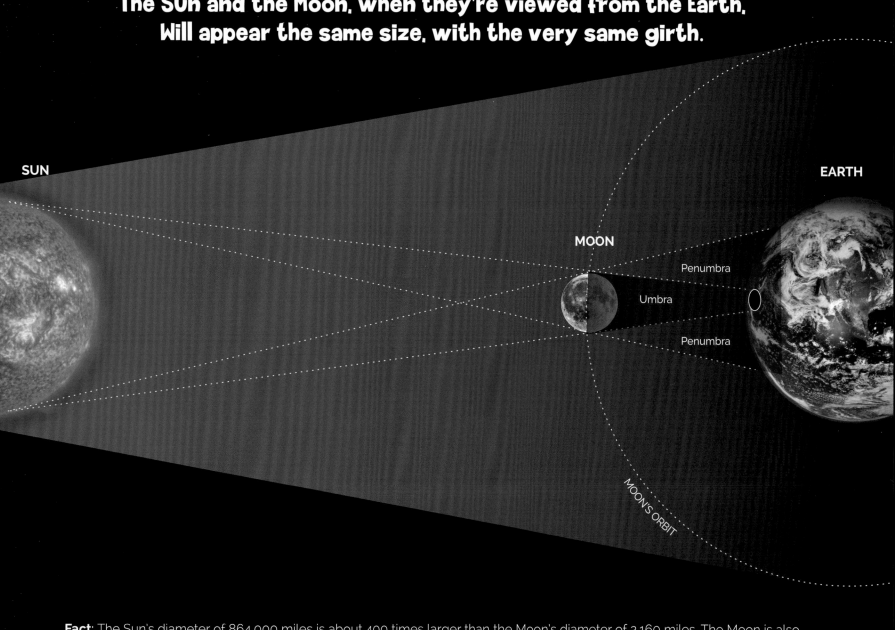

The Sun and the Moon, when they're viewed from the Earth, Will appear the same size, with the very same girth.

SUN

MOON

EARTH

Penumbra

Umbra

Penumbra

MOON'S ORBIT

Fact: The Sun's diameter of 864,000 miles is about 400 times larger than the Moon's diameter of 2,160 miles. The Moon is also about 400 times closer than the Sun. This lucky coincidence means that the Sun and the Moon both look very similar in size when viewed from the Earth, so that when the Moon passes in front of the Sun, it blocks some of the Sun's light from reaching Earth.

And now we will show you just what a New Moon is
And why it's important to solar eclipses.

PHASES OF THE MOON

Full
Moon

Waning
Gibbous

Third
Quarter

Waning
Crescent

Fact: The Moon's orbital period and rotational periods are the same (about 27 1/2 days), so the same side of the Moon, sometimes called the "near side," is always facing us on Earth. During a New Moon, no sunlight at all reaches the "near side."

**Invisible New Moons are able to bite
Off a chunk of the Sun and then blot out its light.**

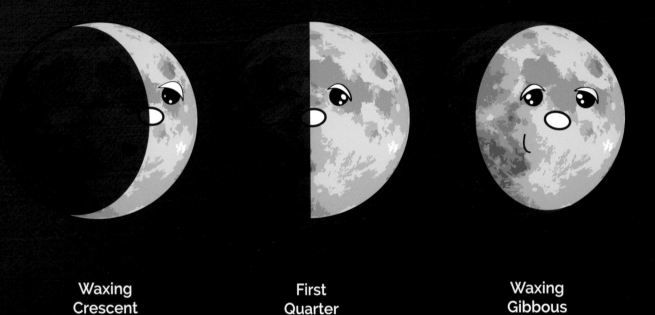

| New Moon | Waxing Crescent | First Quarter | Waxing Gibbous |

Fact: The fact that the New Moon is unlit by the Sun and therefore invisible during the day helps to explain why ancient peoples did not realize that the Moon was about to "sneak up" on the Sun and hide it from view.

We'd how like to mention a couple of things:
And show how eclipses make two kind of rings.

TYPES OF SOLAR ECLIPSES

PARTIAL SOLAR ECLIPSE

The Moon does not fully cover the Sun's disk. **You won't see a ring**, and instead The Sun will appear as a crescent of various sizes. **But remember: you must never look directly at The Sun during a partial eclipse!**

ANNULAR SOLAR ECLIPSE

The Moon appears slightly smaller than the Sun, so a **"Ring of Fire"** is visible around the outside of the Moon. **The same rules apply to viewing an Annular Eclipse as a partial eclipse. Don't look directly at The Sun!**

TOTAL SOLAR ECLIPSE

The Sun and the Moon line up perfectly! The Moon completely covers the Sun, creating, for a few seconds only, what looks like a **"Diamond Ring"**. When the Sun is completely covered, it is safe to view the eclipse without eclipse glasses.

The eclipse we call Annular's fun to admire; The Sun's rim turns into a bright Ring of Fire.

Fact: An annular solar eclipse happens when the Moon passes between the Sun and Earth at or near the farthest point in Moon's orbit, called the "lunar apogee." The Moon, being farther from Earth, appears a little bit smaller than the Sun. Instead of completely covering the Sun's disk, the Moon's position allows a ring of light, called an "annulus," to appear around it. The kind of shadow this produces is called an "antumbra."

A total eclipse is a marvelous thing:
And its midpoint is gorgeous: a bright Diamond Ring!

PHASES OF A TOTAL SOLAR ECLIPSE

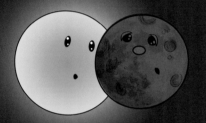 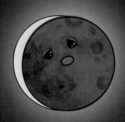   

1st CONTACT

The eclipse begins as the Moon starts to overlap the edge of the Sun.

2nd CONTACT

The Moon almost covers the entire Sun with only a sliver of its edge peeking out

TOTALITY

The Sun is completely covered and only the Sun's atmosphere can be seen.

3rd CONTACT

The Moon continues on its way past the Sun, and the Sun's disk begins to reappear.

4th CONTACT

The Sun is almost entirely visible again marking the end of the eclipse.

Totality truly is nothing to fear.
It's a chance to observe the Sun's bright atmosphere.

CORONA

CHROMOSPHERE

Fact: The Sun's atmosphere has two layers: the chromosphere and the corona. The solar atmosphere is usually not visible to us as it is outshone by the light emitted by the bright yellow surface of the sun, called the photosphere. The chromosphere is a pinkish red layer of hot jets of gas. The Corona, which is hundreds of times hotter than the photosphere, extends far out into space, and from it comes the solar wind that travels through our solar system at speeds as high as one million miles per hour!

Fact: The Diamond Ring Effect lasts only for a few seconds at most at the beginning and end of totality. "Beads" of sunlight, called Baily's Beads, will shine through some of the ridges and valleys on the Moon's rim. The last of these will look like a brilliant diamond set in the ring of corona surrounding the hidden Sun.

Partial eclipses can also be fun
As you look at the Moon while it nibbles the Sun.

Fact: A partial solar eclipse occurs when the Sun, Moon, and Earth are not perfectly lined up, so the Sun's disk won't be completely covered by the Moon. The Sun will look like a half, quarter or crescent moon. In addition, during a total or annular solar eclipse, people within the penumbra, the partially shaded area outside the umbra (or the antumbra in the case of an annular eclipse), will also see a partial solar eclipse.

**And if you're not in the path of totality?
A partial eclipse has its own personality!**

A partial solar eclipse is seen as the Sun rises over the United States Capitol building, Thursday, June 10, 2021, as viewed from Arlington, Virginia. Although visible as a partial eclipse in the United States, some people in Greenland, Northern Russia, and Canada saw it as an annular eclipse.

Image Credit: NASA/Bill Ingalls

To watch an eclipse there is one basic rule:
You can learn this from books; you can learn it in school:

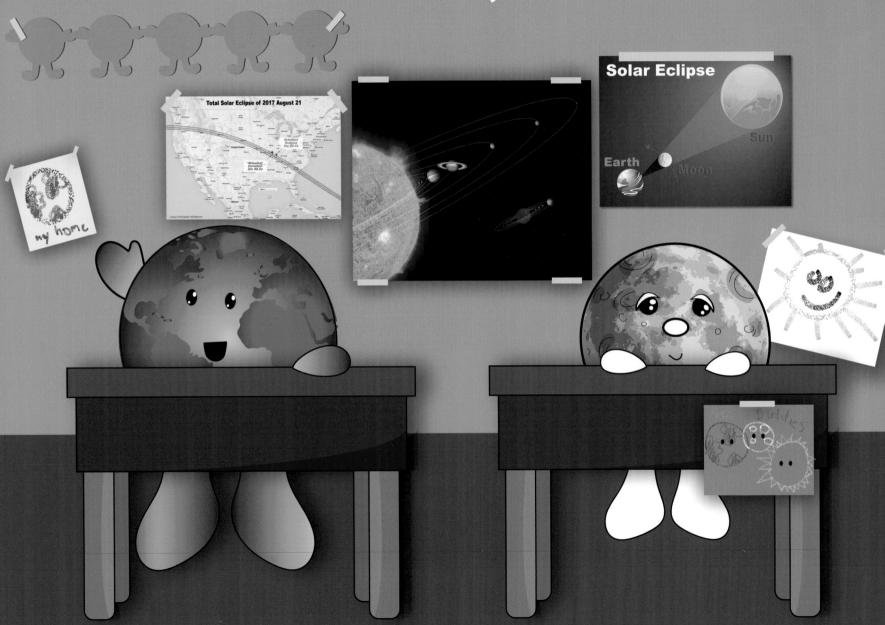

You must never (that's NEVER!) look straight at the Sun!
But with special dark glasses, eclipses are fun.

Without special glasses, we fear that you'll find
That you'll ruin your eyesight, (or even go blind).

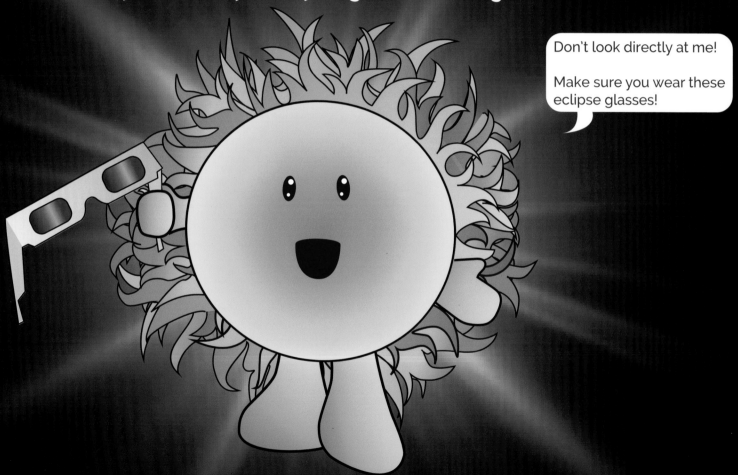

Don't look directly at me!

Make sure you wear these eclipse glasses!

Fact: Your Buddies don't want to scare you, but we do want you to enjoy eclipse viewing safely. Looking directly at the Sun is dangerous to your eyes, but with these very dark special glasses, made according to international safety standards, you won't have to worry.

For partial eclipses you MUST wear our glasses.
That's our advice, and it also is NASA's.

Astronomers certainly know what they're doing.
So use our great glasses for safe eclipse viewing.

Although Special Glasses like ours are quite nice,
A "Camera Obscura" will also suffice.

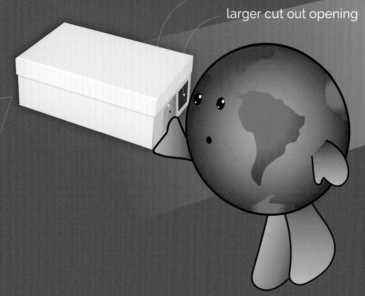

small hole made in aluminum foil

larger cut out opening

what you see!

TIPS:
If you don't have special glasses you can make a pinhole camera to safely view the eclipse.

HOW TO BUILD A PINHOLE CAMERA (OR SOLAR VIEWER)

Fact: A camera obscura is a darkened room or box with a small hole or lens at one side through which an image is projected onto a wall opposite the hole. This "pinhole camera" is a kind of camera obscura.

YOU WILL NEED:	ASSEMBLY:	HOW TO USE:
A cardboard box White copy paper Adhesive tape Aluminum foil The point of a pencil Scissors 	Tape foil on outside of box Make a small hole through the foil and cardboard Cut a larger opening next to foil Tape paper to inside of the box opposite the small hole	Face away from the Sun. Allow the Sun's light to pass through the pinhole View through the larger opening A small image of the eclipsed Sun will be visible opposite the pinhole

But now's your best chance, so you better not wait:
It's October 14 or it's next April 8!

Fact: An annular eclipse will be visible from North Central to Southeastern United States and into South America on October 14, 2023. The total eclipse of April 8, 2024 will extend from Mexico and Southwestern United States through New England and into Canada. **For both eclipses, people in all 50 states will experience at least a partial eclipse!**

Mark your calendars now; it's best not to tempt fate.
If you don't make plans early, you could be too late.

OCTOBER 14, 2023 PATH OF ANNULARITY

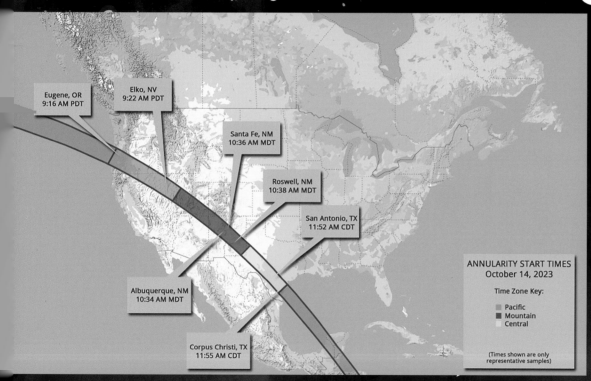

Eugene, OR
9:16 AM PDT

Elko, NV
9:22 AM PDT

Santa Fe, NM
10:36 AM MDT

Roswell, NM
10:38 AM MDT

San Antonio, TX
11:52 AM CDT

Albuquerque, NM
10:34 AM MDT

Corpus Christi, TX
11:55 AM CDT

ANNULARITY START TIMES
October 14, 2023

Time Zone Key:

■ Pacific
■ Mountain
□ Central

(Times shown are only
representative samples)

See the
Ring of Fire!

Fact: More than 6 million people live within the "path of annularity" of the October 14, 2023 Annular Eclipse, and anyone living in any of the 50 states will experience at least a partial eclipse.

Map courtesy of NationalEclipse.com, Map adapted by NationalEclipse.com from original at eclipse.gsfc.NASA.gov. Map copyright Google. INEGI. Eclipse Predictions Courtesy of Fred Espenak, NASA/Goddard Space Flight Center.

Note: NationalEclipse.com has very detailed and informative individual maps and lists showing precisely where and when an annular eclipse can be observed in each state along the path of annularity.

After these two (if you live in the States), it's two more whole decades until the next dates!

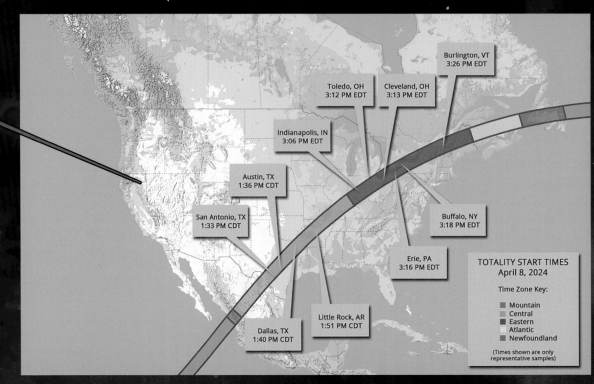

APRIL 8, 2024 PATH OF TOTALITY

Burlington, VT
3:26 PM EDT

Toledo, OH
3:12 PM EDT

Cleveland, OH
3:13 PM EDT

Indianapolis, IN
3:06 PM EDT

Austin, TX
1:36 PM CDT

San Antonio, TX
1:33 PM CDT

Buffalo, NY
3:18 PM EDT

Erie, PA
3:16 PM EDT

Little Rock, AR
1:51 PM CDT

Dallas, TX
1:40 PM CDT

TOTALITY START TIMES
April 8, 2024

Time Zone Key:
- Mountain
- Central
- Eastern
- Atlantic
- Newfoundland

(Times shown are only representative samples)

Fact: More than 30 million people live within the path of totality of the total eclipse of April 8, 2024, and many more are likely to travel there to see it. The duration of totality could be as long as 4 1/2 minutes. . .almost double that of the Great American Eclipse of 2017! No matter where you live in the United States, however, you will experience at least a partial eclipse!

Map courtesy of NationalEclipse.com, Map adapted by NationalEclipse.com from original at eclipse.gsfc.NASA.gov. Map copyright Google. INEGI. Eclipse Predictions Courtesy of Fred Espenak, NASA/Goddard Space Flight Center.

Note: NationalEclipse.com has very detailed and informative individual maps and lists showing precisely where totality can be observed in each state along the path of totality. https://nationaleclipse.com/maps.html

Make your plans soon, and please don't hesitate.
If you miss out on these, it's a very long wait!

Map courtesy of NationalEclipse.com. Map adapted by NationalEclipse.com from original at eclipse.gsfc.NASA.gov. Map copyright Google. INEGI. Eclipse Predictions Courtesy of Fred Espenak, NASA/Goddard Space Flight Center.

Fact: Although several more total eclipses will be seen in the United States during the 21st century, the next ones, after 2024, won't be until 2044 and 2045!

Oh, what a joy is a Solar Eclipse!
And now that we gave you our "How-to-View" tips.

And now that the cause of eclipses is known;
And now that your knowledge about them has grown;

And now that you've seen all the pictures we've shown...
We hope that you'll see an eclipse of your own!

Glossary
A Guide to the Meaning of Some Terms Mentioned in this Book

Annular Eclipse: An annular solar eclipse happens when the Moon is at or near apogee, that is, when it is somewhat farther from the Earth than during a total eclipse. It covers the Sun's center but leaves the Sun's visible outer edges to form a "ring of fire" or "annulus" (Latin for "ring") around the Moon.

Antumbra: From Latin, meaning "before the shadow," the antumbra is the area of shadow where you can see the Moon entirely within the Sun's disc, blocking much of the Sun's light, but not blocking the "Ring of Fire" that appears around the Moon's rim. An observer in this region will see an annular eclipse.

Astronomy and Astronomer: Astronomy is a natural science that studies celestial objects and phenomena using mathematics, physics, and chemistry in order to explain their origin and evolution. Objects of interest include planets, moons, stars, nebulae, galaxies, and comets. More generally, astronomy studies everything that originates beyond Earth's atmosphere, and an astronomer is a scientist who specializes in astronomy.

Baily's Beads: Related to the "Diamond Ring" phenomenon, Baily's Beads are a feature of total and annular solar eclipses. As the Moon covers the Sun during a solar eclipse, the mountains and valleys on the Moon allow "beads" of sunlight to shine through in some places while not in others. The effect is named after Francis Baily, who explained the phenomenon in 1836.

Chromosphere: A thin reddish layer surrounding the photosphere of a star, such as our Sun. The Sun's chromosphere can be briefly glimpsed during a total solar eclipse.

Corona: The Sun's corona lies outside the chromosphere and extends millions of miles into space. It is most easily seen during a total solar eclipse and is hundreds of times hotter than the surface of the Sun, which is known as the photosphere.

Diamond Ring: The diamond ring effect is seen when only one Baily's Bead is left, appearing as a shining "diamond" set in a bright ring around the Moon.